Poetry Of Everything Book 2
By Lord R.e Taylor

Dedication

I do hereby, by the power invested to me by the universe, dedicate this book of poetry to everything, everybody, and every place in our ever-expanding universe which inspires poets, artists, songwriters, authors, and actors to create such beauty in the world.

Published by Shadowlight Publishing

Ipswich, Queensland, Australia

© 2024

All rights to all written material enclosed are reserved for Shadowlight Publishing and/or Lord R.e. Taylor

Nothing may be reproduced without written permission from Shadowlight Publishing and/or Lord R.e. Taylor

ISBN: 978-1-7636761-1-4 "print"

ISBN: 978-1-7636761-2-1 "kindle"

A Closed Door

I had better be careful
I cannot let my imagination loose
It doesn't take a lot
Even just a closed door can fire it
So many stories locked away
So many possibilities hidden inside
And they will not let me know
So, my heart races beyond control
My mind swirls making my head explode
All because of a closed-door
And a really warped mind

Walking Barefoot

One day
Not too far off
A promise will be kept
The Sun will be in the right place
Not too close and not too far away
The clouds will be hiding from view
And for a moment the world will stop
There will be no work or worries
And you will have the time you want
On that day throw your shoes away
You won't need them
Walk through a field of flowers
Or along a warm sandy beach
Just let your feet know that you are alive
And see where they take you

Pains Of Morning

Morning comes too soon
Disturbing my restless sleep
I feel it dragging me into the day
Of course, I want to resist
My time in bed is too important
But it always manages to win
So, it leads me into a world of confusion
And stresses I could never imagine
Still, without the morning light
The best of my world would never be seen
That moment when your eyes open
When you look at me and smile
That makes it all worth the pain

Remember A Better Life

Remember a time when being a kid was fun
You could play outside and not have to worry
If you got hurt, you just walked it off
You took chances which you knew were stupid
But it was all in the name of having fun
Even if you did get hurt there was always a band-aid at home
And your mom sent you right back out
That perfect life was sixty years ago
Kids today are not allowed to play
They are not allowed to get hurt
They live their lives wrapped in bubble wrap
And that is no life at all

Paradise In A Valley

The field opened up
Surrounded by trees
Framed by majestic mountains
People have dreamed of such a place
Written songs and poetry
Tributes to nature's beauty
Someday man will find this place
With all of their problems
That field may not survive
For now, it is still a paradise
Hopefully, it always will be

Missing Mommy

Mommy, Mommy it has been forever
We have a thousand hugs saved for you
Maybe more if you want them
Just hurry home PLEASE

Adulting

Being an adult can be hard
In fact, it really sucks
So many demand so much
Never giving you time to rest
Nothing is ever good enough
So, you keep trying
Wanting to do more and more
Having to do more and more
It can become too much though
But we never give up
We fight on
That is all part of being an adult

My Flame Is Out

The candle was lit the day I was born
It's light never faded
Lasting as long as I have
It has seen me through so much
Every bad time and every good time
But now that candle's light has died
I do not have the body or soul any longer
So, just as the last wisps of smoke leave the candle
I leave my world behind for all of you
I wish you luck with it

His Prayer

He never knew when you left
Never knew where you went
All he knew was that his heart was empty
He cried through the night
A prayer flows between his tears
One prayer that fills his soul
Asking for just a few seconds to say goodbye
But, it is a wish that will never be answered

He Took Her Hand

She lost her way long ago
Wandering without hope
She had no hope left
Until a man took her hand
She didn't know He was there
She just felt comfort from His touch

Where Are The Heroes

Watch old-time movies
Men and women were heroes
Where did they go
Wiped away by time
Destroyed by a new reality
If only we could be like that again

The Book Lady

She has seen millions of books
Reading every one of them
Now, she shares her experiences
Showing you the way to new worlds
So, don't just stop by
Take your time and enjoy all of her history

The Way There

A million people
Walk on asphalt and cement paths
Through valleys of glass and steel
They find corners to make a choice
And they only take them to other corners
And more choices
It is an endless circle
Some spend their whole lives
Walking and searching for a magical land
With fields of grass and flowers
Trees making shade in the summer sun
And a lake surrounded by laughing children
To most, it is just a story
A hopeful tale shared by parents
But, for those who search long enough
Persevere through time and space
The oasis in the concrete desert is real
A place of dreams and pleasure
And they will never forget the way there

All You Have To Do Is Look

Life is so hard
Stress at every turn
Wrapping around you
Choking the breath from you
Usually, there is no escape
But there is a chance
Throw off your necktie
Let your suit fall on the floor
And the getaway
Then look around
Find a meadow, forest, or glen
And walk
Walk and listen to the world
Sing along with the birds
And smell the life surrounding you
After the hours or just the moments
Go back home but remember
There is more to life than wearing a suit
More than work or stress
It is all waiting all around you
All you have to do is look

The Beauty of a Wall

Let the vines cover the wall
Hiding all the cracks
The flaws put there by man
Initials carved by ancient lovers
Imperfections of beauty
No one will know of them
No one will see them
They will be forgotten
Lost to time
Lost in the fantasy of perfection
Centuries later the wall has not changed
Has not given in to fashion
The wall still stands alone
Its true beauty is hidden
But it is still there with its imperfections
With a pride that it knows its beauty
It's worth it to the universe
Even if no one ever looks at it
Or sees beneath the vines
It is beautiful

Be Careful Of The Rock You Throw

A rock does not know its own power
Try throwing into the calmest of ponds
Listen for the noise of the splash
Watch the ripples as they travel to the shore
That pond has been changed forever
And it will never be the same again
It is the same with a young child
Say anything either happy or angry
And that child has been changed forever
The splash you hear will be their self-esteem
The ripple that you see will be their pride
So, think of that rock when you speak to a child
Remember that what you do now will make changes
Maybe not today or tomorrow
But the changes will show themselves
Maybe, it will be bad or maybe it will be good
So, watch what you say to that young child
Their future is the rock in your hand
All you need to do is throw it to change their world

The Weeping Angel Of The Forest

She was placed there so long ago
Her job was to protect an ancient forest
But man came in and saw the beauty of the land
The forest was not something they wanted
So, they came in with saws and axes
Cutting down the trees by the hundreds
And when they finished only a very few were left
The angel still watches over her charges
But now her eyes are full of bitter tears
Instead of the life and hope they once held
She will remain in the forest she loves
Surrounded by the children she has protected
Always showing the mourning she feels
She has been given a name which truly fits her
She is The Weeping Angel Of The Forest
And her remaining children are safe as
long as she lives

The Animal In The Cage

Locked in a cage

Steel bars of my own making

The floor lined with the bodies of those who came before

Alongside the bones of those who conspired to harm me

My fingers claw in desperation

Ripping the flesh from the ends

Exposing claws lost eons ago through evolution

My teeth tear into the metal filing my mouth with orange powder, powder that corrodes my throat making it impossible to talk Impossible to scream or plead for my life

Alas, the more I try to escape the smaller the cage becomes

Compressing my hopes and dreams Shrinking any spirit or soul I may have left.

Why would the owner of the cage treat me so? Men, women, and children walk by my cage

Pointing and laughing at the animal trying to escape They must know the pain I am in

Maybe they can see past the hatred I feel

Maybe they can see the torture in my eyes

All they have to do is look

Maybe if just one person looked and saw the real me One bar would fade and I would be released

Maybe I could be human again If only just one person took the time

The time to see that the animal before them was a man

If just...

Elysium Fields

I know that I will die someday
Not sure of when I will be taken
I am even less sure of what will finish me
But I think about where God will send me
Heaven is not a possibility
Hell seems to be a little more likely
I may be a bit too much for them though
Maybe, if I can change enough now
God can send me to a paradise, not His Heaven
Rather a place well-known in ancient times
He may send me across the wide ocean
Allow me to walk through the Elysium Fields
And finally, find some peace

Memories Of Home

When she was a little girl
Two wars filled her streets
Her father served as a POW
Locked in a British prison camp
Disease took so many others
Many she knew
Even with all of that, she was a child
Still, after nearly a century
She remembered Breslau in its beauty
The hometown she left behind

Bad Rhyming Poem

I am sorry if my poems are long
Have to make sure the words are not wrong
But sometimes when the writing is done
Know that there are some meant-to-be fun
So if you laugh please let me know
I may have a thousand more to show
If you all show nothing but frowns
I will have to put my quill pen down
For now, though I must say goodbyes
And I hope tonight that no one dies

The Beauty Of You

I fell in love with you
It has never been easy
You are so beautiful
Out of my class
Still, my heart goes to you
And you were all it ever needed
But even with that, I am trouble
I look at a thousand flowers
Carefully examining each one
Color and petal count
And just the right scent
It is a quest I can never finish
There is no flower in nature
Which is as beautiful as you

Your Dark Clouds

Everyone has the time
When dark clouds fly in
Taking over the mind and heart
Placing happiness in the shadows
Making stories and poems
Different from anything else you have written
Talking of thoughts that shouldn't be thoughts
Actions that should never be done
Those dark clouds will remain
For as long as they desire
There is nothing you can do
Nothing you can say or think
Nothing you can pray for
They will not listen to you
Until you are truly ready for them to leave
Then your happiness will return
And you will once again be you
At least until the dark clouds return again

Nature's Church

Nature opens
The sun shines through
Making a natural church
A place to pray
Thanking God
For the world's beauty

2nd Half Of The Day

The second part of the day
Cooling the world below
Making everything nicer
Allowing relaxation
Waiting for sunset

Dragonfly

In millions of years
Since the world began
Beauty has surrounded us
In the trees and flowers
In the skies and clouds
And in the waters of our seas
The smallest of life has created its own
The beauty of colors in their bodies
And the laciness of their wings
Even the dances they have learned
They have a grace no human could match
Everything created by God's hand
The simple dragonfly is what we have wanted
What we have needed in our lives
Beauty, grace, and a melody seen forever
But, rarely ever noticed

Broken Mirror

He looks at his broken mirror
A lonely, sad man
Who lost hope a long time ago
But he sees a hundred visions before him
Different versions of himself
Ones he could never see before
Maybe there is one among the hundred
One that may give him hope
And an idea of how to improve his life
He just needs to look at everything he is
And everything he has to offer
Hopefully, he may find what he needs
Hiding in the shards of broken glass
And he can fix his broken life

Born To Destroy

He was born of wind, lightning, and thunder
Raised by the darkness of Hell
He knew what the world could be
Nobody is laughing or smiling
Contagious hatred spreads like wildfire
No one ever stood a chance to escape
So, the world ended in pain and torture
And he just stood and laughed
Pleased that he did what he was born to do

The Light Of Stars

At the moment the sun sets
He gathered the light from the rising stars
Placing them around the bed of a princess
Just so you will not fear the darkness

"Your" Creations

It used to be a challenge
Trying to be creative
But those days are sadly gone
Now it may take a little talent
A few minutes of time
And the right computer program
With just the right keystrokes
You can be an artist, a poet, or even an author
Or maybe you can be all three
Remember though, your creations will not be yours
They will always belong to a computer chip
Shared with millions of other "creative people"
Each one "thinks" they are an artist, poet, or author
on their own
But all are just pretenders not the same as you
No matter how many keys they press

Jesus

He was born of a poor family
In a Jewish town in a Jewish land
He grew up to preach the Gospel
Travelling the land helping people
Making miracles when He needed to
He became a very famous man
Called the King of the Jews
In the end He was murdered by a foreign land
After giving the world His body and blood
Yet, His teachings will never be forgotten
The memory of Him dying on the cross
He answers so many prayers
Proves that He never truly died
And that His love still guides us all

Fading Day

I thought I was crazy
So, did everyone I know
Leaving my life behind
Wandering the world
Out of all eternity
Looking for that one moment
The one which showed a beauty
Beauty which no one knew existed
But I did find it
Hidden in an Arctic snow field
The moment when the endless day ends
And the endless night begins
A moment of fading beauty
Which will never be remembered
But should never be forgotten

When You Wish Upon A Star

My mother always told me
When you have a wish to make
Wish it upon a distant star
Look for the brightest one
And, once I am gone, it will be me
Waiting in Heaven to hear your voice
I will listen to you and do my best
To hear your wish and grant it for you
But child make sure you know this
I will not grant every one
Only the ones which are good for you
I am your mother after all
And I always know what is best for you
So, my child, have faith
And always look for the brightest star
Cause I will be looking for you

Aokigahara

She didn't know where to go
She had no one to talk to
And problems no one knew of
All alone she wandered the forest
Looking at the trees and flowers
Thinking the entire time
What was she worth
Why didn't anyone care
A length of rope and a steady branch
And she found the peace she needed
A victim of her demons
A guest of the Aokigahara Forest

Growing Up

I refused to grow up
That started so long ago
A family which kept on growing
So many jobs came and went
And pains where pains shouldn't be
But I never did grow up
Now I see people walking with canes
Forgetting what they were doing
They have the same silver tint as I do
And giving up their fave spicy foods
Then it hits me when I talk to them
We are the exact same ages
Some are even younger
I realize the one thing I never wanted to
I DID grow up and there was nothing I could do

Dirty Knees

You don't know it yet
Your time is way too short
Play the way you want to
Run across the meadows
Jump in the summer sun
And let your knees get dirty
You are a little girl
A free spirit
Blessed with energy and excitement
And an innocence to see the world
So be who you are
Your time is short
The day will come when you are grown
With a job and a child
And, on the toughest days
You will remember when you ran and jumped
When you loved getting your knees dirty
And maybe you will smile
When your daughter comes home with dirty knees

Bougainvillea

I almost didn't find you
Hiding in the back of the garden center
Just a stick with a couple of leaves
Something told me you were special
I paid the fifteen bucks they wanted
And you went home with me
A large pot and some deep black soil
And soon you became family
I watered you and cared for you
Made sure that you were never too dry
A year later you had grown
Taken over the garden
But I still loved you
And your pink leaves and tiny flowers
You made my mornings as I looked out
And I knew that life would be good

April 8th

We were warned about what was coming
Floods and earthquakes
Increasing human sacrifice
And so many other curses
All of that is based on ancient myths
Even so, millions of people celebrated
Booking vacations months ahead
Settling anywhere they could find the room
All for a four-minute show only we can see
It will reappear in four years and a world away
But no matter what history tells us
There is nothing bringing doom to us all
Just a solar eclipse made to amaze us
And show us the true beauty of the universe

Creative Child

Parents beware
Let your child be creative
Let them express themselves
But know one thing
If they are painting a flower
And they have use of the paints
If they are left alone for even a moment
They will paint the floor
They will paint the tables
They will paint the walls
And they will paint the chairs
They will make themselves
Every color of the rainbow
As well as some new ones
But nowhere in the room
Nor in the universe will you ever find a flower
Being the great parent, you are
You will tell the child how great it is
And you will clean and dread the next time
When your child gets creative

Be A Girl Again

What happened to the little girl
The one I knew as she grew up
Playing hopscotch all-day
Barbies in the evening
And laughing when someone stepped on a jack
That was the girl who climbed trees
And roughhoused with the boys
She grew up and became a woman
Strong, proud and sure of herself
Inside her though hides that little girl
Who wants to play hopscotch and Barbies
Laughs when someone steps on a jack
And still wants to climb trees and roughhouse
Let her out once in a while and be a girl again

The Magic Of A Dollhouse

Someone bought it two hundred years ago
Just a toy for someone's little girl
A home for her dolls and all of her dreams
Over time the dolls moved out
New little girls saw a new reason for the house
They could see fairies and other magical friends
The girls always knew where their friends were
And who will be there to help them dream
When the nights got too rough or too long
They were always there to wipe away the tears
Over the years the girls created
more and more magic
Every wish and prayer went into the little house
Every one was answered with a piece of hope
And that hope was shared with others
in an endless chain
All because someone bought a toy two hundred
years ago

Eternity Of Nothing

When the daylight turns black
And the light of a new moon cannot be seen
Whispers begin echoing through the air
Voice of souls trapped in the in-between
Neither are they dead nor are they alive
They call out into the night
Screams of torture and pain
Begging for anyone to help them
But that help will never come
They are long-forgotten souls
Not given Heaven or Hell
Just an eternity of nothing

My Diet

Okay, I know what you are thinking
I should not even think about it
But damn it looks so good
You know I have been on a diet
Well, I know it too
But I am really hungry
And it looks very very tempting
Maybe just this once I will scarf it down
Just do not look at me like that
After dieting for one day, I think I deserve it

A Proud Aboriginal

He wasn't very old
Not a child but not yet a man
He lived a good life
But he was doing something wrong
His Mum was black, and his Dad was white
A crime in the eyes of way too many
So, the Government took him away
He was given away to an unknown family
Rich and white
The best Australia has to offer
He was taught how to be white
And taught to forget being black
His culture was lost
The Dreamworld was lost
The language was lost
Still, he lived and grew into manhood
Learning his heritage as he grew
And one day he will return
No longer carrying a European name
He once again will become a proud Aborigine

Travel To Woop Woop

I have heard of a place
Far off the beaten track
It's a place everyone talks about
But no one ever goes there
It ain't on any maps
No one can give you directions
That may be half the fun of going
Pack for snow, rain, heat or flooding
You will never know until you get there
So, get on your way to Woop-Woop
Hopefully, it will still be there for you

Nonconformist

Today, I want not to behave
I don't want to be like you
Working 9 to 5
Then going home and going to sleep
That just isn't me
I want to go up the down escalator
Do a donut in a busy intersection
Maybe eat what I am not supposed to
You can be normal and follow the rules
But I know that isn't me
So, I don't even try
If you can accept who I am
And that I will never be like you
I think we could be friends

Just One Snowflake

It has been a long time
But the memories are still clear
Waking up on a December morn
Squinting as your curtains opened
Just to admire a new blanket of snow
So pure and virginal, never disturbed
It was so totally beautiful
But that was many years ago
Now there are palm trees and high heat
Christmas trips to the beach
And roasting snags under the bright sun
How I pray for just one single snowflake
I watch the skies and my hopes fade
No snow again this year
God, I miss seeing just one snowflake

Trapped By An Inactive Mind

Your mind is hidden in darkness
Thoughts trapped in deep crevasses
Their screams echo through deathly shadows
Attacked and strangled at their every move
The struggle against invisible shackles
Drawing blood as they fight their captor
Demons search for ideas ripping them apart
Stripped skin strewn across an evil world
A world created from depression and mania
Leaving the ideas disemboweled in the frenzied heat
Blood, skin, and guts boil under the demon's breath
Screams of torture and pain fill the void
left by random thoughts
Still alive, they choke on the stale sulfuric air
Waiting to die while hoping to be saved
A quick mind lights the darkness
Giving new life to near dead ideas

The strongest fight while the weakest wither and die
They rise through the darkness
Rising into the light they look back
They see the lost ideas dying beneath them
They care about what was lost
What ideas will never see the light of day
And they grieve as they come to light
And they will be told and retold
For that is what ideas are meant to be
Shared by the entire world not killed
Murdered by an inactive mind

Give The Earth A Chance

The world is ending
So, everybody says
Too many people
Breathing and living
Lunatics take to the street
Yelling and screaming
We have to do something
Yet, they are so, so wrong
The world is not ending
We are not going extinct
And everything will be fine
All you have to do is shut your mouth
Stop all your grandstanding
And give the Earth a chance
It can do more to heal itself
Than you could ever think of doing

Forget The Warnings

All your life you heard
Be careful
Don't get hurt
Now, you remember the warnings
But it is so hard to listen
You know you want to do it
Place your foot on the board
And take the first step
You know that you have the ballocks
So, ignore your past
Forget all of the warnings
And just take a chance
After all...
What's the worst that could happen

The Unholy Four

We are the Unholy Four
Together since kindie
Our lives are intertwined
We eat together, drink together
And got into trouble together
Life would not be life without them

Grab A Drink

The world has stopped smiling
Everyone hates everybody
And no one talks
The time has finally come
For one moment
Everyone grab a drink
Wine, whiskey or beer
And toast the person next to you
Say hello
Wish them a good day and smile
If we all do that just once
What a happy world this would be

Her Window

I knew that old woman
The one you lived behind the window
Every morning, she would give me a cookie
I would chow it down while she watered her plants
Now those curtains never open
She is gone but that window, it was her life

Make Everyone Listen

Little one
You were born not long ago
So much like your father
Wise beyond your years
Brave as any warrior
Just take your time
Be patient with others
But always use your voice
Howl as loud as you can
For the life of the pack
And for yourself
Don't you ever stop
Make everyone listen

I'll Always Love You

Ever since that night, you left
I have cried so often
My eyes have dried
But I cannot stop loving you
I am not sure is a blessing
Or is it a curse that I deserve
I do not know and I do not care
No matter what has happened
Or whatever may happen
You will always fill my heart
And you will always be in my mind
I will always love you

Do Not Mourn Us

Please do not morn for us
We were the best we could be
Maybe we were not good enough
So, please do not mourn for us
It is far too late now

A Weary Warrior

His sword lies on the ground
He has been a warrior all his life
Fighting so many battles
But never attaining anything
He has tried to improve his life
But there was always another obstacle
Still, he kept fighting
He never gave up the fight
Finally, his mind has given up on him
His body could no longer rise to fight
Still, he lived the way he thought he should
Now his battles are over
His wars are finished
And now is his time to rest

Please Sit With Me

Please come and sit with me
You don't have to talk
But, I hope that you will listen
I have lived for so many years
And I have seen so much
And lived a life you could never imagine
Let me tell you about my darkness
And let me share my light with you
I will tell you of the people I loved
And the ones who left me behind
I just want someone to remember
So, please come and sit with me
You don't have to talk
But I hope that you will listen

Loss Of A Country

Dig, dig, dig
Deeper and wider
Take the cities
Take the villages
And take the rainforests
Take the Aboriginals
The Europeans
And the Asians
Put them in your hole
Make them dig for you
Looking for gold and uranium
Dig down as far as you can go
Dig to the shores of the mighty oceans
Make it so the land no longer exists
Only a hole where a country used to be
Then what will you do

Charon

When I close my eyes
I can feel my heartbeat
It feels so very strange
Most everything is gone
But Charon I can see you
How long have you been watching me
Just waiting for my last-second
I would love to travel with you
Cross the River Styx beside you
If that is to be my fate
I will board the ferry with a smile
If my fate is to not stand with you
Then please wait for me
I promise I will return to you
Carrying two silver coins
My fare for Hades's Ferryman

30 Years Gone

30 years have passed since I last
gazed into your eyes
Then your eyes were filled with love
Many times, I held your hand and kissed you but
something kept us apart
Something would not let me show
all of my love for you.
It burned in my heart, but the fates would
not allow it to happen.
Now time has brought you back to me
and my heart soars as it never did before.
I smile from a mouth that has not smiled in years
My eyes sparkle more than the night sky
in the clear desert air.
The sound of your voice is lighter and carries
a tone of laughter that has been missing
It is you Elliana who makes me young
and lets me dream of what could be.
Every word you speak proves that there is a heaven
and that someday I will be able to share
my love with you.
Finally, be able to spend the rest of my life where I
should have been by your side forever and a day.

Cajun Pride

Remembering an autumn day
Floating down the river
Where all his tensions flow away
And the days just become a blur
The current is always so mellow
And the shore is beauty beyond compare
Lined by age-old weeping willows
It is the answer to a river boy's prayer
The bayou is a special place
Full of stories of old
Told slowly and never apace
They are things the river boy will always hold
As he floats beyond the oldest willow
He looks into the heavens
And he sees his grandpa lying on his pillow
And he remembers his pride in being Cajun

Open Beauty

Sometimes, somewhere
A beauty is created
A beauty never seen before
It could be a natural painting
Or a sculpture created alone
But we are the ones who benefit
The ones who see the miracles
The ones who love nature
And the ones who will protect them

Carpe Noctem

He was born in the darkest of night
There are no lights anywhere to be seen
Even the angels fled to safety
Throughout his whole life, he embraced the night
Hiding from the hatred of light
Demons welcomes him into their home
And he fit in better than he should
No one knew about his desires
No one knew that he feared the light
And the evil world that it created
Even in his moment of death, he rejected the light
His lips formed as the last breath left his body
And you could hear the words "Carpe Noctem"
"Seize the night," the way he lived
And the way he died

Painting Paradise

I know there is a paradise
And I have been looking for it
But I know that I must create it
Make it my own
But I know that I cannot do it alone
I have a brush with but a single hair
Just enough to make a small mark
But not enough to make it real
My heart brought me to you
A woman with a brush like mine
Looking to create your own paradise
Maybe using our brushes together
We can design a place just for us
Our paradise will be born

The Empty Window

More years ago than I want to count
We lived near Kreuz Strasse
There was a little girl who lived there
She was maybe three years old
And she always wore a smile
But she was never outside
We never saw her except through a window
She would wave to us every day
And always mouth "hallo" to each of us
And she was why we always walked that way
Then, the soldiers came
We kept walking by and one day she was gone
No one told us what happened
But we missed that little girl and her smiles
Seventy-five years later I still stand before the house
Staring up at that empty window
Looking for a smile that will never return

Angels In The Country

I don't know where I'm going
And I don't know where I've been
I've been wandering this country
From the Ridge to the Eastern Coast
Meeting so many people
Each so different from the others
I never found any anger or hatred
Just people who said "hi" and shared a cuppa
Every land has its own cultures
None were better or worse than the others
They all just lived the way they wanted to live
Maybe when my journey ends
I will share my stories about those I met
And, if someone listens
They will learn that the world is magical
And the souls living here are the real angels
When they hear me the world may survive
And the angels will be the only people we see

Hidden You

Everyone sees you
No one sees the real you
You are hidden behind a mask
One that you created long ago
Maybe it was to protect you
Maybe it was to hide you away
Someday your mask may fall
The face paint will fade away
And you will be finally revealed
We may get to know you
We may get to know how you feel
And what do you think
Until then we will still see you
And only when you are ready
We will see the real you
The best you there can be

What Have You Done To Me

What have you done to me?
I have known since I met you
I remember every word you have said
Every movement you have made
And every breath you take
You have taken me over
Controlling my thoughts and dreams
Makes me miss you with everything I am
Making my heartbeat just for you
And your scent fills my every breath
But whatever you do keep doing it
I will never fight it
I am in love with you
And that is all I want to know

You Keep The Rain

You have waited so long
Listening to our prayers
And choosing to ignore them
Our plants withered and died
Grasses turned a deathly shade of brown
And our animals lay dead in the fields
Was it a game for You
Just to see how far You could push us
Well, we stood strong before You
Stronger than You thought we would ever be
Go ahead, keep the rain from us
We know that You can do that
But just so You know
We will be here with or without You
And maybe that will bother You, maybe not
But we don't care anymore, and You don't matter

The Woman Of The Cemetery

Outside an isolated cemetery
A lady walks through a foggy night
Always the same night...May Seventh
She never moves from her path
Always looking straight ahead
She can speak but she has no voice
Even the birds and animals are silent
She is never seen for too long
As you pass and maybe look back for her
She becomes part of the fog
And goes back to her world
Wherever that may be

My Little Baby Girl

You were my little girl
You were to be all sugar and spice
Frilly dresses and Barbie Dolls
That was before you saw real-life
It may have changed you
Some say for the better others for the worse
But, through it all, I still see my sweet baby girl

Purgatory

I felt my last heartbeat
Took my last breath
Then the scream came
My soul no longer belonged to me
Wearing her black robes
She lowered herself from her horse
The Banshee came to collect me
She never spoke, not a single word
But I knew that I had to go
Where I had to go was her decision
She dumped me at the door to the afterlife
I heard family and friends calling from above
Family and friends calling from below
She left me to rot in the land of Purgatory
Her decision and her law without appeal
So, I guess I found my new home
At least for all eternity

A Carefree Walk

I walk the streets
I can see other people
I know that they have problems
Everyone does
But I do not want to hear them
Honestly, I just don't care
I do have my own problems
Certainly, I do
I chose to keep them locked away
Instead, I walk the streets
Feeling the warmth of the sun
Savouring the cool Autumn breeze
As I walk, I leave my worries behind me
And my mind and heart are as carefree
The same as they were when I was born
A million torments ago

A Loving Cup Of Coffee

Seriously, I know you
I know you better than you know yourself
You dream about me every night
And I can wake you anytime I wish
All I must do is just sit back and wait
You do not have any way to get away
You didn't when you brought me into your life
And you don't have a choice now
Just look at you shaking and craving me
But know that I will not tease you forever
I am brown, hot, and creamy
Just the way you like me
The way you have always liked me
I will always satisfy you
All you must do is ask

A Dog Is A Dog

Dogs come in the same colors as humans
White, black, brown, yellow, and red
But they never see it
Everyone is the same to them
There are even dogs of many colors
Still, that does not matter
A dog is a dog is a dog
No differences, just another dog
Just like a human is a human is a human
No differences, just another human

Butterfly Beauty

How did God do it
Gathering every color from everywhere
Finding the ideal brushes
And using the perfect canvases
Not too big and not too small
Even though they do not last too long
Butterflies are works of art
Perfect, beautiful, and graceful
Just what they were created to be

Please Lady Pandora

Beautiful Lady Pandora
I know we have not been perfect
And we do not deserve your grace
But we have survived so much
Going to hell and back
Year after year
Over and over again
Despite everything we survived
The one thing we needed was hope
The hope you saved for us
So please Lady Pandora
Keep hope safe for a little longer
We need it now to save our lives

You Will Never Be Alone

It is so sad what someone did to you
Not wanting to be your mommy
She left you all alone on your special day
Not even giving you a name
She wanted you to be alone for eternity
Little did she know that was not going to happen
It didn't matter how long you were on this Earth
Many celebrated your life and mourned your death
Know that, for as long as you are in our hearts
You will never be alone in Heaven
The angels will make sure of that

Walk The Path

What are you waiting for
It may be the unknown
But you are going to have to decide
Do you take that first step
Or do you just wait and see
The way could lead to Wonderland
A place of more magic than you could imagine
It could also take you back to land you know
Where your normal life goes on every day
The choice is up to you
No one else can make that decision
So, just take that first step
And see what that ragged path can share

Finding Happiness

When you wish upon a star
Wishes are supposed to come true
So many times, I wished for happiness
Dreamed of just laughing and smiling
All for no reason
But my wishes were never answered
They just drifted off into space
Lost forever to infinity
Yet, I still had hope
After looking for a lifetime
I did find a spark of hope
The secret I had been looking for
Living my life for
It was hidden in a secret place
Inside a box of chocolate chip cookies
Just one single cookie with a cold milk
Showed me complete happiness
Happiness, I knew existed but could never find
All I needed to be forever happy
Would be ninety-nine cents for a pack

The Confederate Boy

He never did anything to you
You don't even know his name
Nor do you care to
He never owned a slave
All he did was fight for his country
He was just thirteen when they took him
Barely old enough to shave
But he fought, and he most likely died
For the freedom of his people
And the liberty of his home
Still after so much time
The young boy is hated and cursed
By people who never knew him
Or his story
But he is still a hero
Someone who believed in his land
Someone willing to die defending it
And today that is so rare
He should be a lesson to us all
Instead of being labelled a criminal

The Journey Of A Water Droplet

A single droplet of water
Identical to a trillion others
It flowed through a hundred
Lakes, rivers, and streams
Just to reach the edge of the mighty cliff
It doesn't fight to stay
It knows that it must go over the edge
In an instant, it falls
Crashing onto ancient rocks below
But, that little droplet isn't done yet
It flies upon strong winds
Lifted into the air with a trillion others just like it
When the sun strikes this special droplet
It lights up with an infinite number of colors
And when it sees a little girl
Holding onto her mother's hand
She is looking into the sky
Looking at that tiny water droplet
And she has the biggest smile ever
That made the trip so well worth it

Stupidity

So long ago I did something
It was stupid and I knew that then
And I know it now
But after nearly a lifetime I found you
On Myspace and then on Facebook
You are still the same woman I loved
And the same woman I will always love
Now, I hope I can prove to you
That stupid young man is gone forever
Maybe you will think with your heart
And we will be together again

Indian Summer

Everyone knows it is coming
A few warm days to enjoy the colours
For children Indian Summer
Indian Summer brings Halloween
Adults know it means snow
But for that exact moment
Just admire the beauty around you
It will not come again for a long time

Autumn Colours

I have never seen them
Nor has anyone else
Tiny, magical little creatures
Waiting through the heat of summer
Pacing back and forth
Wearing holes in the ground
Waiting for the first cool breeze of September
They ready themselves for the right moment
Paint buckets by their sides, brushes in hand
When the first breezes of October come
They fly to the cities and forests of the north
Stopping to paint every leaf on every tree
And even though they may only last a short time
Everyone admires their work
And a few who know who they are
Will thank them and wait another year
Just to see their magic once again

Feathered Alarm Clock

Every morning
Hours before the sun rises
You find that time to laugh
That annoying laugh of yours
Just like a feathered alarm clock
Set to make our lives hell
It echoes around the entire land
Waking men, women, and children
No one is safe from you
The thing is you rarely travel alone
Two, three, or even more
All hiding up in the trees
Can you grant us one small wish
Please try and sleep in just once
Maybe until say eight in the morning
We may all like you if you could

Lifeless Library

What did The Fates do
A temple for knowledge
Destroyed in moments
So many pages no one will read
Every book left there to rot
They were all pure treasures
It doesn't matter who wrote them
How old or how rare they were
No book should face such a death
Maybe someday some person will care
All the lost books will be restored
They will have the chance to live again
And a new generation will love them
Hopefully, it will be better than we did

Daffodils And Crocus

I heard a rumour
A little over a month ago
That Spring would finally arrive
The leaves would come back
And the world would be green again
There was a short-lived hope
Warm breezes came in from the south
Grass began to show
Daffodils and crocus began to grow
Then the hope disappears
Lost in a wind blowing in from the north
The newest buds start to grow
Reaching for the sun
Instead, they find a shroud of freezing snow
But, they will fight and they will win
They will see the sun
And they will welcome Spring

Girl With No Name

I know you have a name
You must have been given one
A name that fits you perfectly
One with beauty and intelligence
With grace and endless charm
Still, I hazard to make a guess
My mind cannot find one that is you
Maybe you will tell me, but maybe not
I might not be the man to know you
That, I guess, will be my loss

His Green Heaven

Raised in the desert
Nothing but beige and blue
He imagined another place
Hills of the greenest green
A Heaven he could never reach

Neptune's Daughter

Neptune's daughter
The most beautiful demon ever
Singing her enticing song
Drawing men to their doom
She has no feelings to show
It is just her job
So, she smiles and sings
Waiting for the next ship to appear
And her body count to increase

Sunshine Hunts Me

The dark is my home
Hiding me away
But the sunshine hunts me
Trying to take my soul

My Redheaded Demon

I have known you forever
Or so it seems
But I have heard so much
How redheads can be a terror
Demons sent to punish man
By controlling us with your glance
You love stealing a man's soul
Adding each one to your number of freckles
You have done so much more than that
My heart and my soul have been stolen
However, you never knew the truth
You didn't really steal them
They were never mine to steal
I gave them to you on the day we met
I always loved you my redheaded demon
Maybe, just maybe, you will love me too

Portrait Of A Shameful History

Such a cute little boy
Like so many others
Convicted of a crime
Ripped from his mother's arms
And allowed to live for a while
While his parents were murdered
He heard them scream when they died
They were burned and he never saw them again
He was judged by a barbaric country
It was decided that he was a danger
For merely being who he is
It wasn't known how long he would have lived
If he was also murdered and burned
Or was he given to a German family
All we have is a picture to remember him by
But that is quite enough to make us think
Make us hope that history never happens again

No Map Needed

No matter how hard you look
It doesn't take a map
GPS will not help you in any way
The place you are looking for
Well, it is the most special place on Earth
Treasures no one has ever heard of
And creatures never imagined
All you have to do is discard your maps
Just unplug your computer
Do not think or plan your trip
Let your heart tell you where to go
And you will never be led astray

After I Am Gone

After I am gone
I want no tears
Just laughter
Some Jack Daniels
But not a single tear
Understand!

Insomnia

In the heat of a summer night
Sleeping naked on cotton sheets
Or in the freeze of a winter's night
Covered in as many blankets as possible
Sleep evades a true insomniac
It doesn't matter whether a full moon
Traveling through a billion stars
Or a new moon with no light to cast down
So, we lay on the bed
Not sleeping but not fully awake
So many ideas enter and leave our minds
I also thought about being a better person
Eventually, the time comes to curse the night
And pray for morning to come
Just so we can leave our self-imposed cell
And still know that another night is coming
But maybe if we pray, we will find sleep
Even if just for a few hours

9/11/2001

It did not take long
Three individual moments
Created by lunatics
Following a belief in their prophet
Thousands of people died
A whole lot more were injured
Nothing was solved that morning
All they did that day was cause hatred
Hatred more than any since the 1940s
It spilled out worldwide
Enveloping every country on Earth
And even after twenty-three years
The anger is still there
Can it ever end
Should it ever end
No, it should always be remembered
Just so that it never happens again

A Nonsexual Poem

It was so nice to see
The way it smiled
When it walked by
Its clothes shined in the sun
And it smiled as it looked over
Although their eyes never met
Or never even talked
It had something it liked
And it wanted to know more
It hoped to be able to talk
But it never stopped walking
It never slowed down
And in a moment, it was gone
Except in its memory
It would remember it always
And it would be happy

Precious Coal And Gas

For two hundred years
His family farmed the land
Children were born
Elders had died
Still, the farm remained
Although they owned the land
It could still be given away
The government didn't care
The dollar signs were way too bright
Blinding them to their people's lives
The coal and gas were too precious
Wanted by foreign lands
So, they sold what they never owned
The farmer's tears and fighting wouldn't help
The coal and gas were too precious
So the farmers would have to give up
Some just lost their land
Others lost their lives
But the government created to protect
Well, they never cared
The coal and oil were just too precious

Clock With No Hands

There has to be a single place
Where you may just sit
Somewhere between the land and space
Somewhere time does not have a permit
I want just to sit on a shore and think
With the stress of life left far behind
Where reality rests before me on the brink
A life that everyone has always pined
A land where clocks have no hands
There is no reason to know the time
Because the world has no demands
No conflict and only a peacetime
But that land could not exist
It is only a dream that so many dreams
Someday that dream will be missed
And the peace will be farther away than it seems

A Carefree Walk

I walk the streets
I can see other people
I know that they have problems
Everyone does
But I do not want to hear them
Honestly, I don't care
I do have my problems
Certainly, I do
I chose to keep them locked away
Instead, I walk the streets
Feeling the warmth of the sun
Savouring the cool Autumn breeze
As I walk, I leave my worries behind me
And my mind and heart are as carefree
The same as they were when I was born
A million torments ago

Tommy Baker

Tommy Baker went to a show
At a brothel where he wasn't known
He knew he'd find hell
If his wife, he did tell
On the way poor Tommy fretted
And man that boy he sweated
He was seated in the very back
Bravery was something he lacked
He didn't need to worry though
His wife was the star of the show

A Harlequin's Tear

You have lived as a harlequin
Always smiling and cheerful
You stay behind your make-up
Keeping yourself hidden
Yet, rarely does a glimpse of you shine through
A single tear finds its way through
And we get to see the real you

Double Dog Dare

Being six years old
It is a hard time
New friends to be with
And five words
You didn't want to hear
Your life was going to change forever
"I double dog dare you"
A phrase you never wanted to hear
But one you loved to say
Whether walking on a wall
Eating a bug
Or kissing that little redhead girl
It was all the same
Potentially deadly
Always something you didn't want to do
But you were double dog dared
So, you walked that wall
You ate that bug
And you even kissed that girl
That girl you eventually married
Thank God for double dog dares
They make life exciting

Goodbye And Good Luck

You are just one of the trillions
A mere microscopic insect
Existing on a microscopic planet
There really is no difference
Between you and a bacterium on your skin
So, there is no need to hate other creatures
Just because you are not alike
So, sit down and shut up
Because if the world comes to an end
It will not be anyone's fault
But no matter who you are
No one is going to survive
So, to all the trillions dying on Earth
Goodbye and good luck
That is all anyone can say so accept it

Future King

Raised to be a king
He will fill the role
It lives in his eyes

We Will Watch

We have been watching you
Ever since you stood on two legs
We have taught you so much
Helped you build your world
We even became your gods
But you were different then
You lived with a kind of honor
You fought face to face
For reasons which you believed
Lying and theft were looked down on
And respect ruled the day
Now, you can lie, cheat and steal
You can kill a thousand miles away
And become a king among your people
There is no honor in your lives
That is not what we taught you
And we do not think that you even care
So, we will not be back for a long time
We will watch and we hope you will improve
Only then will you learn how to live
Only then will you fit into the universe

Her Heaven

When she was a little girl
She was told of distant lands
Princes and princesses
Lived in magical lands
Where unicorns roamed the forests
The skies were always blue
Flowers bloomed in every color
And the air always smelled of lilac
A century later that same girl lies on a bed
Fighting for another moment of life
But when her time comes
She steps into another world
The one her mother told her about.
Not an imaginary fairy tale land
Her mother told her of a Heaven
That she created just for her

So Sad The Wall

It is so sad
A place with no color
No life to be found
It is just a sad place where no one goes
Blank as the sky is blue
It waits for someone with a vision
To stumble upon it
And not see what it has become
Rather see what it could be
Put flowers on the wall
Surrounding animals at play
No, let there be children
Let them laugh and enjoy live
Show them as we remember we were
Maybe a heroine to inspire us
With a quote for us to live by
Please do not walk past the wall
It is too sad and too lonely
The wall needs someone to look at it
Smile and say that it is beautiful
Before they too walk away

Trials Of A Parent

Why did I grow up?
I should have known better
My parents suffered
Worrying about life
How to provide for everyone
How to make sure we would learn
Throughout the years I heard them cry
But I also heard them laugh
As the years passed by
Now, I am grown with my own kids
And I have the same worries
And I wonder when I lay down to sleep
How did they make it?
How did they live without their mind burning?
I will never know since I never asked them
But I loved them, and I hope that in future years
My kids will think back and remember
Just as I do now
What parents suffer through to give them a good life
And they know they will know they will get through it
Just like we did so many years before

Eternal Desire

For so many eternities
I have been searching for you
Looking for the feel of your cold touch
The scent of your black blood
As it flows through your veins
A few times I have seen you
But in the blink of my eyes, you were gone
Just a misty dream that can never be caught
Or the darkest nightmare I shouldn't try to
Either way, I know what my heart commands
And I will hunt for you until my final moment
Dreaming of the second we will be one
And I will cease to exist

Death By Music

A new set of headphones
Never used until one night
An old 70's radio station
Van Halen, Motley Crue, and Ozzy
More power than 2024 can handle
At least they died a good death
Just the way good music planned it

Password To My Heart

I have kept to myself
My heart locked away
Avoiding any pain
I was happy with that
Then I met you
With your perfect smile
And your haunting heart
You saw right into me
The locks I set up
Designed to keep you away
But you looked
Saw my deepest secret
And, without a single word
You guessed my heart's password
And you opened the locks
One by one they all fell away
At that moment you entered my soul
And I fall in love with you

Grumpy

She wakes up at 5 a.m.
The kids screaming
Husband can't find his pants
Rain is pouring through the ceiling
And the coffee maker's broke
But, she knows of a holy place
Created by a caring millionaire
A place to relieve her pain
And turn her from Grumpy to Happy
An Espresso Macchiato is just what she needs
And she needs to make it a double
Too bad she has no cash
And her purse is at home where she left it
So, Grumpy she is and Grumpy she will remain
At least until she can borrow the needed $8.50
Then it will be "Thank God" for Starbucks

The Lonely Blue Ball

A lonely blue ball
Orbiting a yellow star
So many creatures live there
All kinds of life wander its surface
Every shape, description or colour
Most of them get along and survive
The most advanced of them
Well, they never learned how
They set up invisible borders
Walls to keep them far apart
There are way too many gods for their good
Teaching conflicting messages of love and hate
And choosing leaders who fan the flames
Wanting more and more power and land
They never cared about their people
People who are just left to die
Still, that blue ball orbits the yellow star
Hoping that someday its creatures will learn
And if that happens and the problems stop
The blue ball will spin with a little more joy
And the universe will finally see what it wanted
The planet. that blue ball, as it was supposed to be

Hidden Nightmares

Nightmares are forever
Hiding in the back of your mind
Watching and learning your fears
Studying your worst memories
Watching and waiting
Looking for the right moment
When you are the weakest
When your defenses are the lowest
Only then will they reveal themselves
Driving you ever closer to insanity's edge
But even though you know they are there
They will fear you if you don't acknowledge them
You tell yourself that you are the stronger
Only then will they cower in their shadows
And maybe you can even get a good night's sleep

I Will Not Be Separate

They want to separate us
By gender
By race
By income
By intellect
By sexuality
By nationality
By religion
By beliefs
So many groups to be controlled
To be kept apart
To belied about the others
So that no one will get along
Still, there will be some who will say
I am not a part of any group
I am a member of them all
I am an individual
And I will not be controlled
By you or anyone else

Tattered Pages

You are a true mystery and an enigma
All wrapped within your pages
No one knows when you were written
Or even who took the time to write you
There is no sense of the travels you had
How many people saw you and read you
Did you make a difference in their lives
Or did you terrorize whole communities
We may never know the legend that is you
But even with all your tattered pages
We are just happy that you are still here
And you will be for as long as we care about you
An unknown part of history that begs to be known

Vampire Cat Bat

I am a vampire cat bat
But never fear
After Halloween
I will be a cat again

www.ingramcontent.com/pod-product-compliance
Lightning Source LLC
Chambersburg PA
CBHW072213070526
44585CB00015B/1319